# CONTENTS

# LAKE CLASSICS

*Great American*
*Short Stories II*

WITHDRAWN

## Hamlin
# GARLAND

Stories retold by C.D. Buchanan
Illustrated by James Balkovek

**LAKE EDUCATION**
Belmont, California

# LAKE CLASSICS

### Great American Short Stories I

Washington Irving, Nathaniel Hawthorne, Mark Twain, Bret Harte, Edgar Allan Poe, Kate Chopin, Willa Cather, Sarah Orne Jewett, Sherwood Anderson, Charles W. Chesnutt

### Great American Short Stories II

Herman Melville, Stephen Crane, Ambrose Bierce, Jack London, Edith Wharton, Charlotte Perkins Gilman, Frank R. Stockton, Hamlin Garland, O. Henry, Richard Harding Davis

### Great British and Irish Short Stories

Arthur Conan Doyle, Saki (H. H. Munro), Rudyard Kipling, Katherine Mansfield, Thomas Hardy, E. M. Forster, Robert Louis Stevenson, H. G. Wells, John Galsworthy, James Joyce

### Great Short Stories from around the World

Guy de Maupassant, Anton Chekhov, Leo Tolstoy, Selma Lagerlöf, Alphonse Daudet, Mori Ogwai, Leopoldo Alas, Rabindranath Tagore, Fyodor Dostoevsky, Honoré de Balzac

Cover and Text Designer: Diann Abbott

Library of Congress Catalog Number: 94-075029
ISBN 1-56103-021-X
Printed in the United States of America
1 9 8 7 6 5 4 3 2 1

# ❧ Lake Classic Short Stories ❧

*"The universe is made of stories, not atoms."*
—Muriel Rukeyser

*"The story's about you."*
—Horace

Everyone loves a good story. It is hard to think of a friendlier introduction to classic literature. For one thing, short stories are *short*—quick to get into and easy to finish. Of all the literary forms, the short story is the least intimidating and the most approachable.

Great literature is an important part of our human heritage. In the belief that this heritage belongs to everyone, *Lake Classic Short Stories* are adapted for today's readers. Lengthy sentences and paragraphs are shortened. Archaic words are replaced. Modern punctuation and spellings are used. Many of the longer stories are abridged. In all the stories, painstaking care has been taken to preserve the author's unique voice.

*Lake Classic Short Stories* have something for everyone. The hundreds of stories in the collection cover a broad terrain of themes, story types, and styles. Literary merit was a deciding factor in story selection. But no story was included unless it was as enjoyable as it was instructive. And special priority was given to stories that shine light on the human condition.

Each book in the *Lake Classic Short Stories* is devoted to the work of a single author. Little-known stories of merit are included with famous old favorites. Taken as a whole, the collected authors and stories make up a rich and diverse sampler of the story-teller's art.

*Lake Classic Short Stories* guarantee a great reading experience. Readers who look for common interests, concerns, and experiences are sure to find them. Readers who bring their own gifts of perception and appreciation to the stories will be doubly rewarded.

# ❦ Hamlin Garland ❧
## (1860–1940)

## About the Author

Hamlin Garland's parents had just moved from Maine to a farm near West Salem, Wisconsin. There, Hamlin was born just before the Civil War broke out. In the years that followed, the family moved from Wisconsin to Iowa and then to the Dakota Territory. But nowhere did they find the success and fortune they had been looking for.

When Garland was 24, he left the frontier to return to the East. His parents' struggles had convinced him that the rural Midwest was not a land of promise and opportunity. In his eyes, it was a land of hardship, poverty, and bitter disappointment. He settled in Boston, where he began to educate himself. He would spend hours in the Boston Public Library. There he studied history, literature, and Darwin's new theories of evolution. In time, he became a teacher and a writer.

His first collection of stories was called *Main-Travelled Roads* (1891). It was reviewed as being "full of the bitter and burning dust, the foul and trampled slush of the common avenues of life."

Garland wanted to show frontier life as it really was—full of hard toil and endless drudgery. "I have lived the life," he said. "I know that farming is not entirely made up of berrying, tossing the new-mown hay, and singing 'The Old Oaken Bucket' on the porch by moonlight."

Garland called his own style of writing "veritism"—a word based on the Latin word for *truth*. He wrote about the harsh and ugly realities of life. His purpose was to expose these realities in order to improve the lives of ordinary working people.

If stories about real life on the American frontier interest you, you'll like Hamlin Garland.

# Under the Lion's Paw

Poor people in all ages have been crushed under the "lion's paw" of power and greed. This famous story shows the author's sympathy for the struggling farmers of 100 years ago. The main character knows that his only chance lies in back-breaking work. But will that be enough to save him?

"Mother, this is Mr. Haskins—from Kansas. His farm's been eaten up by grasshoppers."

# Under the Lion's Paw

## I

The last day of autumn and first day of winter had come together. All day the farmers plowed their prairie fields through clouds of snowflakes. The snow melted as it fell, wetting them to the skin.

Under their dripping harness, the patient horses swung to and fro, to and fro. The wild geese, honking wildly, sailed down the wind and were soon lost to sight.

Snow covered the farmer's coat, and mud sucked at his heavy boots. But he whistled as he worked, as if to drown out the wind.

Then night began to fall. The geese had started landing in the cornfield nearby. But Stephen Council was still at work. He rode the plow when the wind was with him, and walked when he had to face it. Sitting bent and cold, he talked cheerfully to his team.

"Come round there, boys! Round again! We got to finish this land. Come in there, Dan! Steady, Kate, steady! Now, once more!"

The horses seemed to know what he meant—that this was the last round. They worked with even more energy than before.

"Once more, boys, and then, oats and a nice warm stall."

By the time the job was done, it was too dark to see the house. And the snow was changing to rain again. The tired and hungry man could see the light from the kitchen shining through the hedge. "Supper for a half a dozen!" he shouted loudly.

It was eight o'clock by the time he had finished his chores and started for the house. He was carefully picking his way through the mud when the tall form of a man loomed before him.

"What do you want?" the startled farmer cried.

"Well, you see," began the stranger, "we'd like to get in for the night. We've tried every house for the last two miles, but no one has room for us. My wife is getting sick, and the children are cold and hungry—"

"Oh, you want to stay the night, eh?"

"Yes, sir. It would be a big help—"

"Well, I don't usually turn anyone away hungry. Not on nights like this. Drive right in. We don't have much, yet such as it is—"

But the stranger was already bringing his weary horses up past the well. Council stood beside the wagon and helped the stranger's wife and two half-sleeping children climb down.

"There you go!" he shouted to the children. "Now you're all right! Run along to the house there. Tell Mrs. Council that you want some dinner."

"Mother!" he called, as he neared the kitchen. "Here are some folks who need something to eat and a place to sleep." He pushed them all inside.

Mrs. Council was a large, jolly woman. Immediately she took the children in her arms. "Come right in, you little rabbits. Here's a drink of milk for each of you. I'll have some tea in a minute. Here, sit up by the fire."

While his wife fed the children, Council went to the barn to help the stranger with his horses. Mrs. Council put tea and toast on the table. "Don't wait for the men, Mrs.—" She paused, waiting for a name.

"Haskins."

"You eat this right up, Mrs. Haskins. I'll get more bread and milk for the little ones. Don't you move a finger! I know all about taking care of babies!"

Mrs. Haskins, a small, sad-looking woman, was still very pretty. At Mrs. Council's kind words, her eyes filled with tears. Slowly her tears fell down on the baby sleeping in her arms. In the warm kitchen, the world no longer seemed such a cold place to her.

"Yes, it's true. A man can't move a mountain," Council was saying, as he entered the kitchen with the stranger. "Mother, this is Mr. Haskins—from Kansas. His farm's been eaten up by grasshoppers."

Haskins was a tall man, with a thin, gloomy face. His hair was reddish brown, like his coat. Both were faded by the wind and sun. The drooping line of his mouth showed that he had suffered.

After their meal, the women put the children to bed. Haskins and Council talked on, seated near the huge cooking stove. The visitor told the story of his struggle and defeat. It was a terrible story, but he told it quietly. Most of the time he gazed into the fire.

"And the grasshoppers ate you out four years in a row, eh?" Council asked.

"Ate! They wiped us out. They chewed up everything that was green. I think they were waiting for us to die so they could eat us, too. I used to dream of them sitting on the bedpost—six feet long, and working their jaws. They ate the fork-handles. It got worse and worse until those grasshoppers just rolled on one another, and piled up like snow in winter. Well, it's no use! If I talk all winter, I'll still never tell the half of it. That land was just the wrong place for a man to have a farm!"

"Well, why didn't you settle here instead?" Council asked.

"Why, because you fellows wanted 10 to 15 dollars an acre for just the bare land. I had no money for that kind of thing."

"Well, now, I'll tell you," Council said, "I'd go down and see this fellow Butler *anyway*, if I was you. He might let you have his place pretty cheap, since the farm's all run down. Butler's been wanting to rent to someone next year. It would be a good chance for you. Anyhow, you go to bed now and sleep. I've got some plowing you can do, and we'll see what else we can think of. Ike, you go out and check on the horses. I'll show the folks to bed."

Soon the tired husband and wife were lying under the warm blankets of the spare bed. Before drifting off to sleep, Haskins listened for a moment to the wind outside. Then he said to his wife, "There are people in this world who are good enough to be angels. They only have to die to *be* angels."

## II

Jim Butler had started his working life in the grocery business. He had a small store in the poor part of town. He worked very hard, earning every penny he got. But after two years, he had changed. That was when he sold a lot of land for four times what he had paid for it.

From then on, he believed in buying and selling land as the surest way to get rich. Every cent he had was spent on land that people were forced to sell. He would simply buy up their mortgages. Of course, that meant he only had to pay the amount of money that was still owed. Usually, he could pay off the land by harvesting just one crop of wheat.

Farm after farm fell into his hands. He held mortgages on land all over Cedar County. As the owners fell behind on their payments, Butler would first take over the farms. Then he would usually rent the farm back to its former owner. In this way he kept ownership of the land himself. And of course he kept the rent that the former owner paid him to stay there.

"I don't want your land," Butler would say. "All I'm after is the interest on my money. Now, if you want to stay on the farm—why, I'll give you a good chance. I can't have the land lying vacant." In many cases, the owner felt that he had no choice. He stayed on as a renter because he couldn't afford to start over again somewhere else.

Butler had sold his store. He had no time to spend in it now. He had gotten used to sitting around town on rainy days talking with his friends. Sometimes he just rode to and fro from his farms. In spring and summer he fished a great deal. He traveled all over Wisconsin on hunting trips. But in spite of the 20 farms he owned, he was careful to make people think that he was poor.

A fine farm, known as the Higley place, had fallen into his hands last year. It had come to him in the usual way. So far he had not been able to find a tenant for it. Poor Higley had worked himself nearly to death on it, trying to pay off the mortgage. Then he finally gave up and went off to Dakota. That left his farm to Butler.

This was the farm that Council told Haskins about. The next day Council hitched up his team and drove downtown to see Butler.

"Now you let me do all the talking," he said to Haskins. "Don't let Butler think you *want* that place. He'll sock it to you hot and heavy if you look anxious. You just keep quiet. I'll fix him."

They found Butler sitting in Ben Ashley's store. He was telling fishing stories when Council strolled in.

"Hello, Butler. Lying again, eh?"

"Hello, Steve! How goes it?"

"Oh, so-so. Too much rain these days. I thought it was going to freeze up for good last night. I'll be lucky to get my plowing done. How's farming with you these days?

"Bad. Plowing not half done."

"Got anyone working the Higley place?"

"No. Know of anybody?"

"Well, no—not exactly. I've got a friend back in Michigan who *might* come if he could get a good set-up. What do you want for the farm?"

"Well, I don't know. I'm willing to rent it for shares of the crops. Or I'll always take money."

"Well, how much money?"

"Say, ten percent of the selling price. Now let me see, that would come to about $250."

"That's not too bad. Would you wait for your money until after he thrashes?"

Haskins listened eagerly to this important question. Council, however, was calmly eating an apple. Butler studied him carefully.

"That would cost me $25 of my interest money."

"My friend will need all he's got just to get his crops in," Council said, cool as you please.

"Well, then, all right. I guess it wouldn't hurt to wait." Butler decided.

"All right. This is the man. Haskins, this is Mr. Butler, the hardest-working fellow in Cedar County."

On the way home, Haskins thought about the deal. "I'm not much better off," he said. "I like that farm. It's a good farm—but it's all run down, and so am I. I could *make* a good farm of it if I had any money. But I can't stock it nor seed it."

"Well, now, don't you worry," roared Council in his ear. "We'll pull you through somehow till harvest. Butler's agreed to pay you for plowing. You can earn a hundred dollars doing that. The seed you can get from me, and pay me back when you can."

Haskins was silent while he struggled with his feelings. At last he said, "I have no money to live on."

"Now, don't you worry about that either. You just stay with us. Mother Council will be happy to have your wife and children around. Our daughter's married, you know, and our son's away a lot. So we'll be glad to have you stay with us this winter. Next spring we'll see if you can get started again."

"Say, Council, you can't do this. I never saw—"

"Hold on, now," said Council. "Don't make such a fuss over a little thing. When I see a man down, I just like to help him up. That's what I believe in."

They rode the rest of the way in silence. When they neared the lights of Council's house, Haskins thought of his family. It made him happy to know they were warm and safe inside. He could have hugged Steve Council. But all he could say was, "You'll get your pay for this some day, Steve Council."

"Don't want any pay. That's not the way I believe."

### III

Haskins worked like a madman, and his wife did the same. They rose early and worked without stop until dark. When they fell into bed, every bone and muscle was aching. Then they rose with the sun the next morning to begin again.

Their oldest boy drove a team all through the spring, plowing and seeding. He milked the cows and did countless other chores.

By June of the first year, the result of their work began to show. The farm's yard was cleaned up and planted in grass. The garden was plowed and planted.

Council had given them four of his cows. Other men had sold him tools on time payments. Haskins began to look forward to the future. After he had rented the farm for three years, he could rent it again or buy it.

Council said, "If you have a good crop, you can pay your debts. Then you can keep your own seed and bread."

The new hope that sprang up in the Haskins family grew stronger day by day. Every day Haskins would grab a few moments after supper to stand outside. There he would look at his wide field of wheat. His heart was filled with joy.

The harvest came. Oh, how they worked! Clothing dripping with sweat, arms aching, fingers raw and bleeding, backs breaking under heavy loads, Haskins and his helper worked on. Tommy drove the harvester while Haskins and another helper bound the wheat. In this way they cut ten acres every day. Almost every night Haskins returned to the field after supper. There he would stack his grain by the light of the moon. He was often still at work at ten o'clock at night.

His wife cooked for the men. She took care of the children, washed and ironed, milked the cows, and made the butter. Sometimes she fed the horses and watered them while her husband kept at the harvest.

Haskins drove himself at his work gladly. He was working for his family. Every day he felt that he was getting nearer to a home of his own. Every night he felt that he had pushed need a little farther from his door.

It was the memory of having no home that drove Tim and Nettie Haskins to such fierce labor.

## IV

"Well, yes. Well, yes. First rate!" said Butler. His eye took in Haskins' neat garden, the pig-pen, and the well-filled barnyard. "You've done all right, haven't you?"

"Yes, and I've put out quite a good bit of money over the last three years. Why, just the fencing alone cost me more than $300."

"I see, I see," said Butler, while Haskins talked on.

"The kitchen there cost about $200. The barn didn't cost much money, but I've put a lot of time on it. I've dug a new well, and I—"

"Yes, yes, I see. You've done well. Your farm animals alone are worth $1,000," said Butler. He shifted from foot to foot and picked his teeth with a straw.

"About that," said Haskins, modestly. "We're starting to feel like we're getting a home for ourselves. But we've worked hard, I tell you—and we feel it, too. We're kind of planning a trip back to see Nettie's folks, after all of the fall plowing's done."

"Exactly!" said Butler, who seemed to be thinking of something else. "I suppose you're kind of planning to stay here three more years?"

"Well, yes. I think I can buy the farm this fall if you'll give me good terms."

"Um. What do you call good terms?"

"Well, say a fourth down and three years to pay off the rest."

Butler looked at the huge stacks of wheat that filled the yard. He smiled in an odd way. "Oh, I won't be hard on you. How much did you expect to pay for the place?"

"Why, about what you offered it to me for before. About $2,500, or *possibly* $3,000."

"This farm is worth $5,500," said Butler in a firm voice. He didn't bat an eye.

"What!" Haskins almost shrieked. "What's that? Over $5,000? Why, that's *double* what you offered it for three years ago."

"Of course—and it's worth it. It was all run down then. Now it's in good shape. You've spent $1,500 fixing it up. You said so yourself."

"But *you* had nothing to do with that. It's my work and my money that did it!"

"Yes, it was. But it's my land."

"But what's to pay me for all my improvements?"

"Haven't you had the use of them?" replied Butler, smiling calmly.

Haskins felt like a man who had been hit on the head with a sandbag. He couldn't think. He babbled, "But . . . I'd never get the use. . . You'd rob me! You agreed. . .You promised that I could buy or rent the land at the end of three years at . . ."

"That's right. But I didn't say I'd let you take away the improvements. I didn't even say that I'd go on renting the farm at $250. The land is doubled in value. It doesn't matter how it doubled. Now you have three choices. You can pay me $500 a year to rent the farm, or you can buy the farm for $5,500, or you and your family can get out."

Haskins shouted, "But you've done *nothing* to improve this farm. You haven't added a cent. I put it all there myself, expecting to buy. I worked to improve it. I was working for myself and the children—"

"Well, why didn't you buy when I first offered to sell? What are you kicking about?"

"I'm kicking about paying you twice for my own things—my own fences, my own kitchen, my own garden."

Butler laughed. "You *are* green, young fellow. The law will see things a different way, I promise you."

"But I trusted your word!"

"Never trust *anybody*, my friend. Besides, I didn't promise *not* to do this. Why, don't look at me like that! I'm no thief. It's the law! Everybody does it."

"I don't care if they do," Haskins sputtered. "It's stealing just the same. I'll give you $3,000 of my money—the work of my hands and my wife's. That's my offer and it stands."

Butler sneered. "Well, I won't take it. You can go on just as you've been doing. Or you can give me $1,000 down, and a mortgage at ten percent for the rest."

Haskins sat down to think. Slowly it came to him that he was under the lion's paw. The power of the strongest animal was just too great. There was no way out—a poor man didn't have a chance.

Butler strolled around, humming a little tune. He acted like a man politely waiting for the answer to a polite question.

In his mind, Haskins again felt the rain in his face and the mud under his plow. He felt the dust and dirt of the threshing. He thought of the hard work of the last three years. He pictured his wife cooking and baking, without rest.

"Well, what do you think of my offer?" Butler asked in a cool voice.

"I think you're a thief and a liar!" shouted Haskins. Then he leaped up. He grabbed a pitchfork, and whirled it in the air. "You'll never rob another man!" he yelled, his eyes blazing fire.

Butler shrank back, expecting to be hit with the fork. But suddenly, Haskins heard a child laugh. And then he saw the golden head of his baby girl, as she tottered across the dooryard. His hands opened. The fork fell to the ground. His head lowered.

"Make out your deed and mortgage and get off my land. Don't you ever cross

my line again. If you do, I'll kill you,"
Butler shouted.

Trembling, Butler backed away from
Haskins. Climbing into his buggy as fast
as he could, he drove off down the road.
Haskins sat wordless on the sunny piles
of wheat, his head sunk into his hands.

# The Return of a Private

What would it be like to come home after years away at war? Is the man who returns the same as the man who left? Is his home the same? This thoughtful story is set in the first day of a soldier's homecoming.

THE THOUGHT OF DINNER AT HOME BROUGHT A DREAMY
SMILE TO PRIVATE SMITH'S THIN FACE.

# The Return of a Private

## I

The nearer the train drew to La Crosse, the quieter the little group of "vets" became. On the long way north from New Orleans, they had joked and talked. When they had entered Wisconsin, they cheered loudly. They cheered again when they reached the city of Madison. But after that, they hardly spoke. Now there were only four or five left who were going to La Crosse County.

Three of the thin young men were brown from the sun. The fourth was pale. He looked ill, and showed signs of fever. One man limped. All of them had the large, bright eyes of men who had been starved.

There were no bands greeting these returning Union soldiers. No one was there to shout "Bravo!" at any of the train stations. The people who were meeting other travelers looked at the soldiers without interest. This group was the last of the army to come home. People were used to seeing soldiers in ragged blue uniforms, coming home from the war.

The train jogged forward slowly. It was nearly two o'clock in the morning when the engine whistled "down brakes."

All of the men were farmers whose homes were several miles beyond the town. All were poor.

"Now, boys," said Private Smith, the pale one with fever. "We've landed in La Crosse at night. We've got to stay somewhere till morning. Now I ain't got no two dollars to waste on a hotel. I've got a wife and children to feed, so I'm going to roost on a bench. That'll save me the cost of a bed."

"Same here," put in one of the other men. "It's going to be mighty hard to find a dollar these days."

Smith went on, "Then at daybreak we'll start for home—at least, I will."

The station was empty, cold, and dark. Dimly lit by oil lamps, the dirty waiting room was not inviting. But the men prepared to camp on the floor and benches. Tenderly, they spread their own blankets on a bench for Smith.

Private Smith felt sick at heart. He lay there on his hard bed, thinking about his life. Weariness was his only feeling. Now the joy of coming home was mixed with bitter worry. He saw himself, sick and worn out, starting again to work his half-cleared farm. The money he owed on the land would swallow half his earnings. He had given three years of his life for hardly any pay, and now—what?

Morning dawned at last. The four men stood outside gazing at the river and the hills.

"Looks natural, don't it?" one man said, as he came out.

"That it does," Smith agreed. "And it looks *good*. Do you see that peak? My farm's just beyond that. Now, if I can only catch a ride, I'll be home by dinner-time."

"I'm thinking about breakfast!" said one of the others.

"I guess it's one more meal of hardtack for me," said Smith. He pulled out one of the hard, dry biscuits the army had given them.

Then they found a restaurant, where they got some hot coffee. It would help to wash down their hardtack.

Private Smith held up a piece of the hardtack. "One day we'll find it hard to believe that we ever ate this stuff," he said.

"It can't come soon enough for me," cried one. "I've had enough hardtack to last me forever! Right now, I'd like some of the hot biscuits my wife makes!"

"Well, if you sit there all day talking, you'll never see your wife."

"Come on," said Private Smith.

Shouldering their blankets and guns, the men struck out on their last march. For some miles, they kept together on the road by the river. The river was very lovely, curving down along its sandy beds. Under a tangle of wild grapevines, the men sat down to rest. The beautiful scene brought joy to their hearts. But soon it was time to trudge along again, under a sun that grew hotter and hotter.

"Ain't it odd that we don't see any teams of horses on the road?" said Smith, after a long silence.

"Well, no, not when you think of it. It's Sunday."

"Why, that's a fact! It *is* Sunday. I'll get home in time for dinner, sure! She don't have dinner usually till about one on Sundays!" The thought of dinner at home brought a dreamy smile to Private Smith's thin face.

"Well, I'll get home about six o'clock. That's when the boys are milking the cows," said Jim Cranby. "I'll step into the barn, and then I'll say, *'Hey!* Why ain't this milking been done before this time of day?' And then won't they yell!"

Smith went on. "I'll just go up the path. Old Rover will come down the road to meet me. He won't bark. He'll know me. He'll come down wagging his tail and showing his teeth. That's his way of laughing. Then I'll walk up to the kitchen door, and I'll say, 'How about dinner for a hungry man!' And then she'll jump up, and—"

He couldn't go on. His voice choked at the thought of it. Saunders, the third man, said not a word. He had lost his wife the first year he was in the army. While she was working in the fields, she got caught in the autumn rains. Soon after that, she had fallen ill and died.

They plodded along until at last they came to a parting of the ways.

"Well, boys," said Smith, "here's where we shake hands. We've marched together a good many miles. Now I suppose we're done."

"Yes, I don't think we'll do any more of it for a while. I don't want to, I know."

"I hope I'll see you once in a while, boys—to talk over old times."

"Of course," said Saunders, whose voice trembled a little. "It ain't like anybody's dying." They all laughed but still they found it hard to look at each other.

"Maybe we ought to go home with you," said Cranby to Smith. "You'll never climb that ridge with all them things on your back."

"Oh, I'm all right! Don't worry about me. Every step takes me nearer home, you see. Well, good-by now, boys."

They shook hands. "Good-by. Good luck!"

"Same to you. Let me know how you find things at home."

"Good-by."

"Good-by."

Private Smith turned once and waved his cap. The others did the same, and they all yelled. Then they marched away. The lone climber in blue walked on, thinking. His mind was filled with the kindness of his friends. He remembered the many days and nights they had spent together in camp and field.

Then Smith thought of his pal, Billy Tripp. Poor Billy! A bullet had struck him in the chest one day. Tore a great ragged hole in his heart. Smith knew he would have to talk to Billy's mother and sweetheart. They would want to know all about it. He tried to think of all that Billy had said, but there was not much to remember. There had just been a dull slap, a short groan, and the sight of the boy lying with his face in the dirt. That was all. But nothing dimmed the horror of that moment, when his friend fell. Poor handsome Billy! Worth millions of dollars, was his young life.

These sad thoughts changed to more cheerful feelings as Private Smith came nearer to his home. The fields and houses grew familiar. One or two people waved from their doorways. But he was in no mood to talk. He pushed on.

Toward midday, the sun was burning hot and his step grew slower. He sat down several times to rest. Then he would get up and step out again onto the rough road. He walked under great trees and through dense groves of oaks. He crawled along like some tiny, wingless fly.

When he reached the top of the ridge, he ate some hardtack with wild berries. He sat there for some time after, looking down into his home valley. He saw rolling hills and fields of green and yellow wheat far below. His head drooped. His shoulders took on a tired stoop. His cheekbones showed painfully. "Poor, sad figure!" someone watching might have said. "He is looking down upon his own grave."

## II

On Sundays, in a western wheat harvest, all work in the fields stops. Around the houses, in the shade, the men sit dozing or reading their papers.

But at the Smith farm today, there were no men dozing or reading. Mrs. Smith was alone with her three children. They were Mary, nine; Tommy, six; and little Ted, just past four. Her farm, rented to a neighbor, lay at the head of a narrow gully.

The chickens awakened her as usual that Sunday morning. She had been dreaming of her husband. For weeks she had not heard from him. Now the chickens ran around her feet as she went into the yard. Fuzzy little chicks swarmed out from the coops.

A cow called out in a deep moo. A calf answered from a pen nearby, and a pig scurried out of the cabbages. Mrs. Smith stood still and stared at the pig in the cabbages and the tangle of grass in the garden. Then, noticing the broken fence that she had mended again and again, the little woman sat down and cried. The bright Sunday morning was painful without her husband.

They had bought this farm just a few years ago. They paid part of the price in cash and borrowed the rest. Edward Smith was a man of great energy. He worked night and day to clear the land and to pay what he owed.

Then came the call for men to fight in the war. For love of his country, he threw down his farm tools and became a blue-coated soldier. After that he was part of a huge machine meant for killing men instead of weeds. This brave man had left his young wife and three babies behind on an unpaid-for farm. It was a terrible thing to do—but noble, nevertheless.

That was three years ago, and now the young wife felt bitter. It seemed to her that she had carried more than her share of the country's sorrow. Two of her brothers had been killed. One year the farm had been without crops. And now the ripe wheat was waiting to be cut. But the neighbor who had rented her farm was cutting his own wheat first.

About six weeks before, she had received a letter saying, "We'll be home in a little while." But no other word had come from her husband. She had seen other soldiers slowly trickling back in blue streams. But still *her* hero had not come home.

Each week she had told the children that he was coming. Her eyes were always fixed on the road as she stood at the well, or by the kitchen door,

Neighbors said, "He's sick, maybe, and can't start north just yet. He'll come along one of these days."

"Why don't he write?" was her question. But nobody had an answer. This Sunday morning it seemed to her that she could not stand it longer. The house seemed too lonely to bear. So she dressed the little ones in their best home-made clothes and closed up the house. Then she set off for old Mother Gray's.

Mother Gray was a widow with a large family of strong boys and laughing girls. She was a kind woman. Though poor, she fed every mouth that asked for food. And she worked as cheerfully as her daughters danced at the harvest dances.

Mother Gray ran down the path to meet Mrs. Smith. A broad smile lit her face.

"Oh, you little dears! Come right to Granny. Give me a kiss! Come right in, Mrs. Smith. How are you, anyway? Nice morning! Come in and sit down."

The house rang with noise. There were sounds of singing, laughter, whistling, and merry-making. Half-grown boys came to the door and called to the children, who then ran out to join in the fun.

"Don't suppose you've heard from Ed?"

Mrs. Smith shook her head

"He'll turn up one day real soon—when you ain't looking for him." The kind soul had said that many times before. Today, Mrs. Smith could no longer believe her friend's words.

"Now come out and see my new cheese," Mrs. Gray went on. "I don't believe I ever made a better one. If your Ed should come, I want you to take him a piece of it."

In Mrs. Gray's happy, loving household, Mrs. Smith slowly forgot her worries. For now, at least, she laughed and sang along with all the rest.

Soon a wagon-load of people drove up to the door. Bill Gray, the widow's oldest son, piled out with his whole family. Everyone talked at once.

"Ain't heard nothing of Ed, I suppose?" Bill asked, in a loud bellow. Mrs. Smith shook her head.

"I hear two or three of our boys are on their way home. They left New Orleans some time this week. I didn't hear nothing about Ed—but 'no news is good news,' mother always says."

"Well, go take care of your horses," said Mrs. Gray to Bill. "And bring me in some potatoes. Sim, you go see if you can find some corn. Sadie, you put on the water to boil. Come on, now, hurry along, all of you! If I have to put on dinner for this crowd, we've got to have some food in the house!"

The children went off into the fields. The older girls put dinner on to boil, and then went to change their dresses. "We might have some company," they said.

"I hope not! I don't know where I'd put them," Mrs. Gray laughed, pretending to be upset.

When all was ready, Mrs. Smith said, "Now, Mrs. Gray, I shouldn't stay for dinner. You've got—"

"Now you sit right down! If any company comes, they'll have to take what's left, that's all. No, you're going to stay if the whole family starves. And there ain't no danger of that!"

At one o'clock the long table was piled with food. There were boiled potatoes, platters of corn on the cob, squash and pumpkin pies, hot biscuits, sweet pickles, bread and butter, and honey. One of the girls called everyone in to dinner.

A few children came running out of the forest of corn. More came out of the creek, out of the barn, and out of the garden.

Soon the table was crowded with people. "Now dig in, Mrs. Smith," said Mrs. Gray. "You know how these men and boys are! They'll eat up every bite, if you give them a chance."

One by one the men cleaned off their plates and shoved their chairs back. One by one the children finished, too. By two o'clock, the women alone sat around the table, sipping tea. From the tea leaves, Mrs. Gray would tell fortunes.

As each woman finished drinking her tea, she twirled the tea leaves at the bottom of the cup. Then she handed the cup to Mrs. Gray, who peered closely at the leaves.

Mrs. Smith was trembling with excitement when Mrs. Gray began to read her fortune from the leaves.

"Somebody is coming to you," Mrs. Gray said. "He's got a gun on his back. He's a soldier. He's almost here. See?"

She pointed at two little tea leaves, damp against the side of the cup. The tea leaves *did* look a bit like a man with a gun on his back. Mrs. Smith grew pale. She shook so hard that she could hardly hold the cup.

"It's Ed!" cried the old woman. "He's on his way home. There he is now!" She waved toward the road. They rushed to the door to look.

A man in a blue coat, carrying a gun on his back, was climbing up the hill. His bent head was half hidden by a heavy backpack. He was so eager to get home that he would not look aside.

Laughing and crying, the young wife tried to call to him and the children at the same time. Then she ran out into the yard. But the soldier had disappeared behind a hill. By the time she had found the children, he was too far away to hear her call.

She was still not sure it was her husband. He had not turned his head at their shouts. This seemed very strange. Why didn't he stop to rest at Mother Gray's house? Filled with both hope and doubt, she hurried along after him. She ran as fast as she could push the baby wagon. But the blue-coated figure pushed steadily on, just ahead of her.

When the panting little group came in sight of their gate, they saw him. He was leaning on the rough fence. With his chin in his hands, he gazed at the empty house. His backpack, water bottle, blanket, and gun lay in the grass at his feet.

Private Smith was like a man lost in a dream. His eyes took in the scene. Yet he could hardly believe what he was seeing. There was the rough lawn and the little unpainted house with the field of yellow wheat behind it. He heard the crickets chirping merrily, and saw a cat dozing on the fence.

How peaceful it all was! How far away from all the camps and hospitals and battle lines. It was just a little Wisconsin cabin—but it was the most beautiful thing he had ever seen. How had he ever left it for years of tramping, thirsting, killing?

Trembling, Mrs. Smith hurried up to the fence. The oldest boy ran a little ahead. He would never forget the first sight of that figure, that face. It would always remain in his memory—the return of the private. Now he could only stare at the pale face covered with a ragged beard.

The soldier turned, stood still for a moment, and then cried out.

"Emma!"

"Edward!"

The children stood in a curious row, watching their mother kiss this strange, bearded man. Illness had made the soldier partly deaf. This added to the strangeness of his halting, unsure manner.

Smith then turned to his youngest child. He said, "Come here, my little man. Don't you know me?" But the small boy backed away under the fence.

He saw that the war had come between him and his baby. He was only a ragged stranger to his youngest son.

Then the private drew his oldest boy to him. "Tom here will come and see me. *He* knows his poor old dad when he comes home from the war." The mother heard the pain in her husband's voice. She hurried to explain, "You've changed so, Ed. How can he know you? This is papa, Teddy. Come and kiss him. Come, won't you?" But Teddy still peered through the fence, well out of reach.

The soldier sat down to open his backpack. He took out three large red apples. After giving one to each of the older children, he said, "*Now* I guess he'll come. Eh, my little man? Come over here and see your pa."

Teddy crept slowly under the fence, into his father's arms. Then they all entered the house and walked into the poor, bare sitting room.

"Emma, I'm all tired out," said Private Smith. He flung himself down on the rag carpet, just as he used to do. His wife brought a pillow to put under his head. The children stood about, munching their apples.

"Tommy, you run and get me some wood for the stove. Mary, you get the teakettle on. I'll go and make some biscuit," said the wife.

How the soldier talked! Question after question poured out. He asked about the crops, the cattle, the renter, the neighbors. He slipped the heavy shoes off his blistered feet. Then he just lay there in deep, sweet rest. He was a free man again, no longer a soldier at the army's command.

At supper he stopped once, listened, and smiled. "That's old Spot. I know her voice. I suppose that's her calf, out there in the pen. I can't milk her tonight. But I'd like a drink of her milk. What's become of old Rover?"

"He died last winter." There was a moment of sadness in the room. It was some time before the husband spoke again. His voice trembled a little.

"Poor old fellow! He'd have known me half a mile away. I expected him to meet me. It would have been more like coming home to see him running down the road, wagging his tail. I tell you, it was a shock to see the blinds down and the house shut up."

"But you see, we—we expected you'd write again before you started. And then we thought we'd see you if you *did* come," she explained.

"Well, I ain't so good at writing. Besides, it's just as well you didn't know when I was coming. I tell you, it sounds good to hear the chickens out there, and the turkeys, and the crickets. They don't have the same kind of crickets down South. Who's Sam hired to help cut your wheat?"

"The Ramsey boys."

"Looks like a good crop. But I'm afraid I can't do much to get it cut. This fever has got me down pretty low. I don't know when I'll get rid of it. I tell you, these biscuits taste good, Emma. Say, I wish you could have heard me bragging to the boys about your butter and biscuits! Your ears would have burned!"

The private's wife blushed. "Oh, you always did brag about me. But, *everybody* makes good biscuits."

"One more cup of tea, Mary. That's my girl! I'm feeling better already. I believe the biggest trouble with me is, I'm *starved*."

It was a delicious hour, one long to be remembered. But the young wife grew sad when he showed her where he had been struck. One ball had burned the back of his hand. One had cut away a lock of hair, and one had passed through his leg. The wife thought with horror that she might have been a soldier's widow. Her waiting no longer seemed so hard. This sweet hour erased it all.

At last they all went out into the garden and down to the barn. Private Smith stood beside his wife while she milked old Spot. They began to plan fields and crops for next year.

His farm was filled with weeds. It still had to be paid for. The renter had stolen his machinery. His children needed clothes. He was growing older. He was sick and bone thin. But his heroic soul did not falter. He had had great courage when he had faced the Southern march.

Now, with that same courage, he entered upon a still more difficult future.

The pale man with big eyes leaned against the well, his young wife by his side. The children snuggled into their father's arms, and Teddy fell asleep there. Under a golden moon, the crickets called.

The soldier had returned. His war with the South was over. But his fight, his daily fight to make a living for his family, had just begun again.

# Mrs. Ripley's Trip

Some acts of rebellion are private and personal. In this charming story, an overworked farm woman makes good on a promise she made to herself. Her family is shocked by what she intends to do. Will she have the nerve to do it anyway?

"I AIN'T BEEN AWAY FROM THIS HOUSE TO STAY
OVERNIGHT FOR 13 YEARS!"

# Mrs. Ripley's Trip

It was a windy night in November. Cold rain slapped down on the poor little shanty on the vast Iowa prairie. Inside, Ethan Ripley was mending his old violin. His tireless old wife had finished the supper dishes. Now she was knitting a stocking for their little grandson, who lay before the stove like a cat. The old people worked by the light of a tallow candle. They couldn't afford "none of them newfangled lamps." It was a home where poverty was a never-absent guest.

The old lady looked pitifully small and shriveled in her shapeless dress. Yet tonight there was a peculiar sparkle in her little dark eyes. Suddenly she paused and stuck a knitting needle in the knob of hair at the back of her head. Then she made a decisive statement. "Ethan Ripley, you'll have to do your own cooking from now on to New Year's. I'm going back to New York State."

The old man's leather-brown face stiffened into a look of surprise. Then he cackled, "Ho! Ho! Har! Sure you are!"

"Well, you'll find out."

"Going to start tomorrow, mother?"

"No, sir, I ain't. But I am on Thursday. I want to get to Sally's by Sunday, sure, and then on to Silas's on Thanksgiving."

There was a note in the old woman's voice that amazed Ripley. Of course, his first thought was about the money.

"How do you expect to get the money, mother? Somebody died and left you a fortune?"

"Never you mind where I get the money. The land knows, if I'd a-waited for you to pay my way—"

"You needn't twit me about being poor, old woman," said Ripley, flaming up. "I've done my part to get along. I've worked day in and day out—"

"Oh! I ain't done no work, have I?" she snapped. She pointed a knitting needle at him.

"I didn't say you hadn't done no work."

"Yes, you did!"

"I didn't neither. I said—"

"I *know* what you said."

"I said I'd done *my part*!" roared the husband. "I didn't say you hadn't done your part," he added.

"I know you didn't *say* it—but you meant it," she said. "I don't know what you call doing my part, Ethan Ripley. But if cooking for a drove of harvest hands, taking care of the eggs and butter, and digging potatoes and milking ain't *my* part—I don't never expect to do my part.

"You might as well know it. I'm 60 years old, and I've never had a day to myself, not even the Fourth of July. I ain't been away from this house to stay overnight for 13 years. It was the same in Davis County for 10 years before that. For 23 years, Ethan Ripley, I've stuck right to the stove and churn. Not a day or a night off." Her voice choked, but she went right on. "And now I'm a-going back to New York State."

Ethan stared at her in speechless surprise.

"For 23 years, I've just about promised myself every year I'd go back and see my folks." Her voice took on a wistful tone. "I've wanted to go back and see the old folks, and the hills where we played. I've wanted to eat apples off the old tree down by the well. I've had those trees and hills in my mind for many and many a day. Nights, too. And the girls I used to know, and my own folks—"

She fell into a silence that lasted a long time. Slowly, the ticking of the clock grew as loud as a gong in the man's ears. The wind outside sounded drearier than usual. He returned to the money problem.

"But how you going to raise the money? I ain't got no extra cash. By the time the mortgage interest is paid, we ain't got no hundred dollars to spare, Jane."

"Well, don't you lay awake nights studying on where I'm a-going to get the money," the old woman declared. It was clear that she took delight in her secret. She had him now, and he couldn't escape. He showed his indifference by playing a tune on the violin.

"Come, Tukey, you better be off to bed now," Mrs. Ripley said a half-hour later. When she came back from the boy's bedroom, she spoke again. "Pa, you'd better fix that clock. The string for the alarm is broken. I need to get up extra early tomorrow. I want to get some sewing done. I can't fix up much, land knows, but there's a little I can do. I want to look decent."

"You appear to think, mother, that I'm against your going."

"Well, it kind of seems you ain't done much to help me get off."

He felt he was being wronged.

"Well, I'm just as willing for you to go as I am for myself. But if I ain't got no money, I don't see how I'm going to send—"

"I don't want you to *send*. Nobody asked you to, Ethan Ripley. Think what I've earned since we came on this farm! If I had had that much, I'd have enough to go to Jericho."

Then she got up and went to mix her bread and set it to rise. He sat by the fire twanging his fiddle softly. He was plainly in a gloomy mood. But the familiar tune he was picking out slowly set him to smiling.

The old man still sat fiddling softly after his wife went off into their stuffy little bedroom. His shaggy head bent lower over his violin. Then he heard her shoes drop—*one, two*. Pretty soon she called out to him.

"Come, Ethan! Put up that squeaking old fiddle and go to bed. You ought to have sense enough not to sit there all night. You're keeping everybody in the house awake."

"You hush up," he retorted. "I'll come when I get ready, not until. I'll be glad when you're gone—"

"Yes, I'm sure of *that*."

With that pleasant good-night, they went off to sleep. Or at least she did, while he lay awake. "Where under the sun is she going to raise that money?" he wondered.

The next day she was up bright and early. Working away, she ignored Ripley. A fixed look of determination was still on her wrinkled little face. She baked a hen, made a pan of doughnuts, and baked a cake.

Ripley thought about his wife's plan all day as he went about his work. It was cold, blustering weather. The wind rustled among the cornstalks with a wild and mournful sound. Alone in the field, the old man was husking corn. His thin body was rigged out in two or three ragged coats. His gloves were missing nearly all the fingers. Toward evening it grew colder and threatened snow. But in spite of it all, he kept his cheerfulness.

Having plenty of time to think matters over, he made a few decisions of his own. "The old woman needs a play-spell," he thought. "I ain't likely to be any richer next year than I am this one. If I wait till I'm able to send her, she'll never go. Maybe if I sell some pigs, I can get enough to send her. I'd kind of counted on eating them pigs made up into sausages. But Tukey and I can manage without 'em. Then there's that buffalo overcoat. I'd kind of counted on having it. But I guess that's got to go too—along with the sausages."

Once he had decided to make these sacrifices, he acted on them at once. His corn rows ran along the road to nearby Cedarville. As his neighbors passed by, he told them about his plans.

It would have softened Jane Ripley's heart if she could have seen him. Working in the corn rows, he bent his back to the piercing cold. The wind made his dim old eyes water. Now and then he had to stop to swing his arms to warm them. And he was hoarse from shouting at the shivering horses.

That night Mrs. Ripley was clearing the dishes. She got to thinking about leaving home the next day. Slowly, she began to soften. Tewksbury, her little grandson, came up and stood beside her.

"Grandma, you ain't going to stay away always, are ye?"

"Why, course not, Tukey. What made you think that?"

"Well, you ain't told us nothing about it. And you kind of look mad."

"Well, I ain't mad. I'm just a-thinking. We've been so poor all these years, I couldn't seem to get started. Now, when I'm most ready to go, I feel kind of strange. As if I could cry."

And cry she did. But hearing Ripley's step on the porch, she quickly dried her eyes and bent to her work again. Ripley came in the door with a big armful of wood. This he rolled into the woodbox with a thundering crash. Then he pulled off his wet, snow-covered clothes and sat down by the fire.

Mrs. Ripley saw that the light brought out a thoughtful look on his face. His hard life had held back the slender flowers of his nature. But there was warm soil hidden in his heart.

"It's snowing like mad," he said, finally. "I guess we'll have a sleigh ride tomorrow. If you must leave, we'll give you a whooping old send-off. Won't we, Tukey?

"I've been a-thinking things over today, mother," he went on. "I've come to see that we *have* been kind of hard on ye, I guess. I'm kind of easy-going. And little Tuke—he's only a child. We ain't considered how you felt."

She didn't appear to be listening, but she was.

"So today, I asked old Hatfield what he'd give me for two of my pigs. Well, the outcome is—I sent to town for some things I figured you'd need. Here's a ticket to Georgetown, and $10. Why, ma, what's up?"

Mrs. Ripley broke down. With her hands all wet with dishwater, she covered her face and sobbed. She felt like kissing him, but she didn't. Tewksbury began to whimper, too. The old man was astonished. His wife had not wept for years—at least not in front of him.

Now she hopped up and dashed into the bedroom. In a moment she returned with a mitten, tied around the wrist. She laid it on the table with a thump. "I don't want your money," she said. "There's enough here to take me where I want to go."

"Thunder and gimpsum root! Where'd you get that?" Mr. Ripley cried. "Did you dig it out of a hole?"

"No, I just saved it—a dime at a time—see?" She turned the mitten out on the table. There were some bills, but mostly silver dimes and quarters.

"Thunder and scissors! Must be two or three hundred dollars there," cried Mr. Ripley.

"There's just $75.30. Just about enough to go back on. Tickets is $55, going and coming. That leaves $20 for other expenses. It'll be plenty enough to get me there and back."

"But it ain't enough for sleeping cars and hotel bills."

"I ain't going on no sleeper. Mrs. Doudney says it's a scandal the way things are on them sleeping cars. I'm going on the old-fashioned cars. There ain't no half-dressed men running around on them."

"But *you* needn't be afraid of them, mother. At your age—"

"There! You needn't throw my age and looks into my face, Ethan Ripley. If I hadn't taken care of *you* so long, I'd look a little more like I did when we married."

Ripley gave up. He was surprised that the idea of the trip had so unsettled his wife's nerves. She was surprised herself.

"And there won't be no hotel bills. I'm taking a chicken and some hard-boiled eggs," she said. "I'm going right through to Georgetown."

"Well, all right. But here's the ticket I got."

"I don't want your ticket."

"But you've got to take it."

"Well, I don't."

"Why, yes, you do. It's bought, and they won't take it back."

"Won't they?" She was staggered again.

"Nope. A ticket sold is a ticket sold, they told me."

"Well, if they won't—"

"You bet they won't."

"I suppose I'll have to use it." That ended it.

They were a familiar sight as they rode to Cedarville next day. As usual, Mrs. Ripley sat up straight and stiff. There wasn't enough snow on the ground for the sleigh, so they rode in the lumber wagon. The old people sat on a board with a quilt over their knees.

Tewksbury lay in the back. There he jounced up and down in the hay. By the time they reached Cedarville, his teeth were chattering. Every muscle ached from the cold. The railway station—which was always too hot or too cold—was hot today. Little Tewksbury was delighted.

"Now get my trunk stamped or fixed, whatever they call it," the old woman said to Ripley. Then she turned to the boy. "Now remember, Tukey, have Granddad kill that big old turkey right before Thanksgiving. Then you run right over to Mrs. Doudney's. She's got an awful tongue—but she can bake a turkey first rate. You can warm up one of them mince pies I baked. I wish ye could be with me, but ye can't. So do the best ye can."

As Ripley returned with the trunk, she said, "Well, now, I've fixed things up the best I could. I've baked enough bread for a week. And Mrs. Doudney has promised to bake for ye."

"I don't like her baking," he said sadly.

"Well, you'll have to stand it till I get back. You'll find a jar of sweet pickles and some applesauce down cellar. You'd better melt some brown sugar for molasses. And for goodness sake, don't eat all them mince pies up right away! And see that Tukey ain't froze going to school. And now you'd better get going for home. Good-bye, and remember about them pies."

As they were riding home, Ripley turned to Tukey. "Did she—ah—kiss you good-bye?" he asked.

"No, sir," piped Tewksbury.

"Thunder! *Didn't* she? She didn't me, neither. I guess she kind of forgot, being so flustered, you know."

* * *

One cold, windy day, Mrs. Stacey was looking out her window. She had just finished cleaning her little house which was about two miles from Cedarville. Now she was trying to make out an odd little figure struggling along the road. It seemed to be an old woman, laden with at least a half-dozen parcels.

"Why! It's Grandma Ripley, just getting back from her trip," Mrs. Stacey cried. "Why! How do you do? Come in. Why! You must be nearly frozen. Let me take off your hat."

"No, thank ye kindly, but I can't stop. I must be getting back to Ripley. I expect that man has let just about everything go to pieces."

"Oh, you must sit down just a minute and warm yourself."

"Well, I will. But I've got to get home by sundown, sure. I don't suppose there's a thing in that house to eat."

"Oh, dear! I wish Stacey was here, so he could take you home. And the boys are at school."

"Don't need any help—if it weren't for these bundles. Maybe I'll just leave some of 'em here. Here! Take one of these apples. I brought them from Lizy Jane's cellar, back in New York State."

Mrs. Stacey bit into the apple. "Oh! They're delicious! You must have had a lovely time."

"Pretty good. But I kept thinking of Ripley and Tukey all the time. I suppose they've had a jolly time of it. Well, as I told Lizy Jane, I've had my spree. Now I've got to get back to work.

"There's no rest for folks like us. I told Lizy Jane them folks in the big houses have Thanksgiving dinner every day. So Thanksgiving don't mean anything to them. But it's different for us poor folks. We make a great to-do if we have a good dinner once a year!

"I saw a big pile of this world, Mrs. Stacey—a pile of it! I didn't think there were so many big houses in all the world as I saw between here and Chicago. Well, I can't sit here gabbing. I must get home to Ripley. He'll want his supper on time."

Soon the little figure was trudging up the road again. She looked like a little snow-fly, a speck on the great prairie. Crawling along with slipping steps, all she could think about was getting home to Ripley and the boy.

Ripley was out in the barn when she came into the house at last. Tewksbury was building a fire in the old cook-stove. With a cry of joy he sprang up and ran to her. She seized his thin little body and kissed his cheek. It did her so much good that she hugged him hard and kissed him again and again.

"Oh, grandma, I'm so glad to see you! We've had an awful time since you've been gone!"

She let him go and looked around. A lot of dirty dishes were on the table. Splotches of pancake batter decorated the stove.

"Well, I should say as much," she agreed, untying her bonnet strings.

When Ripley came in she had on her apron, and the stove was cleaned. The room was swept, and she was elbow-deep in the dish pan. "Hullo, mother! Got back, have ye?"

"I should say it was about time!" she replied, without looking up. "Has the cow dried up yet?" This was her greeting.

Her trip was a fact now. No chance could rob her of it. For 23 years, she had looked forward to it. Now she could look back at it, accomplished. She took up her burden again, never more thinking to lay it down.

# Thinking About
# the Stories

## Under the Lion's Paw

1. Which character in this story do you most admire? Why? Which character do you like the least?

2. Many stories are meant to teach a lesson of some kind. Is the author trying to make a point in this story? What is it?

3. Is there a hero in this story? A villain? Who are they? What did these characters do or say to form your opinion?

## The Return of a Private

1. Who is the main character in this story? Who are one or two of the minor characters? Describe each of these characters in one or two sentences.

2. Some stories are packed with action. In other stories, the key events take place in the minds of the characters. Is this story told more through the characters'

thoughts and feelings? Or is it told more through their outward actions?

3. Suppose that this story was the first chapter in a book of many chapters. What would happen next?

## Mrs. Ripley's Trip

1. How important is the background of the story? Is weather a factor in the story? Is there a war going on or some other unusual circumstance? What influence does the background have on the characters' lives?

2. An author builds the plot around the conflict in a story. In this story, what forces or characters are struggling against each other? How is the conflict finally resolved?

3. Look back at the illustration that introduces this story. What character or characters are pictured? What is happening in the scene? What clues does the picture give you about the time and place of the story?